Name: _____

GL

English Comprehension & Writing

11+ Practice Papers

Victoria Burrill

GALORE PARK
AN HACHETTE UK COMPANY

The Publishers would like to thank the following for permission to reproduce copyright material.

Photo credits
p17 © Huguette Roe/Shutterstock; p43 © Gail Johnson/Shutterstock

Acknowledgements
pp8–10 from *The Railway Children* by E. Nesbit, published in 1906 (public domain); pp18–19 from *The Sea-Wolf* by Jack London, 1904 (public domain); pp27–28 from *One Flew into the Cuckoo's Egg* by Bill Oddie. Copyright © 2008 Bill Oddie. Reproduced by permission of Hodder and Stoughton Limited; pp36–37 from *The Hound of the Baskervilles* by Arthur Conan Doyle, published in 1902 (public domain)

Every effort has been made to trace all copyright holders, but if any have been inadvertently overlooked, the Publishers will be pleased to make the necessary arrangements at the first opportunity.

Although every effort has been made to ensure that website addresses are correct at time of going to press, Galore Park cannot be held responsible for the content of any website mentioned in this book. It is sometimes possible to find a relocated web page by typing in the address of the home page for a website in the URL window of your browser.

Hachette UK's policy is to use papers that are natural, renewable and recyclable products and made from wood grown in well-managed forests and other controlled sources. The logging and manufacturing processes are expected to conform to the environmental regulations of the country of origin.

Orders: **Teachers** please contact Bookpoint Ltd, 130 Park Drive, Milton Park, Abingdon, Oxon OX14 4SE. Telephone: (44) 01235 400555. Email primary@bookpoint.co.uk. Lines are open from 9 a.m. to 5 p.m., Monday to Saturday, with a 24-hour message answering service.

Parents, Tutors please call: 020 3122 6405 (Monday to Friday, 9:30 a.m. to 4.30 p.m.). Email: parentenquiries@galorepark.co.uk

Visit our website at www.galorepark.co.uk for details of other revision guides for Common Entrance, examination papers and Galore Park publications.

ISBN: 978 1 5104 4976 3

Typeset in India
Printed in the UK

A catalogue record for this title is available from the British Library.

Contents and progress record

How to use this book   4

Section	Page	Length (no. Qs)	Timing (mins)	Question type	Score	Time
Paper 1 Foundation level Representing a GL test at an average level of challenge for grammar and independent schools.						
Reading (fiction): *The Railway Children*	8	50	50	Multiple choice	/ 50	:
Writing: Composition and photograph	17	1	20	Standard	/ 15	:
				Total	/ 65	:
Paper 2 Standard level Representing a GL test at a medium level of challenge for grammar and independent schools.						
Reading (fiction): *The Sea-Wolf*	18	50	50	Multiple choice	/ 50	:
Writing: Story and diary entry	26	2	45	Standard	/ 30	:
				Total	/ 80	:
Paper 3 Standard level Representing a GL test at a medium level of challenge for grammar and independent schools.						
Reading (non-fiction): *One Flew into the Cuckoo's Egg*	27	50	50	Multiple choice	/ 50	:
Writing: Article and review	35	2	40	Standard	/ 30	:
				Total	/ 80	:
Paper 4 Advanced level Representing a GL test at a high level of challenge for independent schools.						
Reading (fiction): *The Hound of the Baskervilles*	36	50	70	Standard	/ 67	:
Writing: Photograph and continue a story	43	2	45	Standard	/ 30	:
				Total	/ 97	:

Answers and
Writing guidance grids   45

Go to the Galore Park website to download the free PDF answer sheets to use and re-use as many times as you need: galorepark.co.uk/answersheets

How to use this book

Introduction

These practice papers have been written to provide final preparation for your GL 11+ English test. To give you the best chance of success, Galore Park has worked with 11+ tutors, independent schools' teachers, test writers and specialist authors to create these practice papers.

This book includes four model papers. Each paper is made up of two parts: **reading** and **writing**. Although the GL paper does not include a writing element, many schools do ask you to complete a separate writing task, so we would suggest you complete both parts of these papers to help you fully prepare for the challenges ahead.

The **reading paper** includes:

- a comprehension exercise to test your understanding of a passage of text
- questions to test your spelling skills
- questions to test your punctuation skills
- sentences with missing words to test your grammar skills.

The **writing paper** asks you to create your own text. This task may link to the comprehension passage you have already read or be on a completely different topic.

The papers increase in difficulty from Paper 1 to Paper 4 and all work to a timing that has been typical of GL tests in the past. This is because GL tests can change in difficulty both from year to year and from school to school.

You will find that you are asked to record your answers to the reading parts in a variety of ways:

- choosing a multiple-choice option using a separate answer sheet
- choosing a multiple-choice option, writing this on the paper itself
- writing a complete answer on the paper itself.

You are being given practice in working with these different styles since the tests may come in any of these formats or as an online test. The styles used in the multiple-choice tests are similar to the question styles you will find in the online tests.

As you mark your answers, you will see references to the Galore Park *11+ English Revision Guide*. These references have been included so that you can go straight to some useful revision tips and find extra practice questions for those areas where you would like more help.

Working through the book

The **Contents and progress record** on page 3 helps you to track your scores and timings as you work through the papers.

You may find some of the questions hard, but don't worry – these tests are designed to make you think. Agree with your parents on a good time to take the test and follow the instructions below to prepare for each paper as if you are actually going to sit your Pre-test/11+ English test.

1 Check at the beginning of the paper if you will be recording your answers on an **answer sheet**. If a sheet is required, download it from www.galorepark.co.uk/answersheets and print it out before you begin.
2 Take the test in a quiet room. Set a timer and record your answers as instructed.
3 Note down how long the reading test takes you (you should complete all questions even if you run over the time suggested) and aim to complete the writing tasks to the length you are advised. If possible, complete both tests in one session.
4 Mark the test using the **Answers** and **Writing guidance grids** at the back of the book.
5 Go through the paper again with a friend or parent, talk about the difficult questions and note which parts of the revision guide you are going to review.
6 Discuss how successful you felt you were in the writing task and go through your marks together to find out whether your discussion partner agrees with your assessment, based on the guidance in the **Writing guidance grids**.

The **Answers** can be cut out so that you can mark your papers easily. Do not look at the answers until you have attempted a whole paper.

When you have finished a paper (both reading and writing tests), turn back to the **Contents and progress record** and fill in the boxes. Make sure to write your total number of marks and time taken in the **Score** and **Time** boxes.

If you would like to take further GL-style papers after completing this book, you will find more papers in the Pre-test/11+ English Practice Papers 1 and 2 (see Continue your learning journey on page 7).

Test day tips

Take time to prepare yourself on the day before you go for the test. Remember to take sharpened pencils, an eraser and, if you are allowed, water to maintain your concentration levels and a watch to time yourself.

... and don't forget to have breakfast before you go!

Pre-test and the 11+ entrance exams

This title is part of the Galore Park *Pre-test 11+* series and there are three further *English Practice Paper* titles (see **Continue your learning journey** on page 7).

This series is designed to help you prepare for pre-tests and 11+ entrance exams if you are applying to independent schools. These exams are often the same as those set by local grammar schools.

Pre-tests and 11+ English tests appear in a variety of formats and lengths and it is likely that if you are applying for more than one school, you will encounter more than one style of test. These include:

- Pre-test/11+ entrance exams in different formats from GL, CEM and ISEB
- Pre-test/11+ entrance exams created specifically for particular schools.

As the tests change all the time it can be difficult to predict the questions, making them harder to revise for. If you are taking more than one style of test, review the books in the **Continue your learning journey** section to see which other titles could be helpful to you.

For parents

For your child to get the maximum benefit from these papers, they should complete them in conditions as close as possible to those they will face in the actual test, as described in the **Working through the book** section on page 5.

Working with your child to follow up the revision work suggested in the answers can improve their performance in areas where they are less confident and boost their chances of success.

For teachers and tutors

The timing of all non-writing elements of the papers is the same in this *Practice Paper* book since fast timing isn't generally a feature of GL-style papers.

In advance of pupils reading through the comprehension passage in each test, it is recommended that you remind them that the blocks of questions will focus on meaning or grammar and vocabulary; spelling; and punctuation and that they will act as a guide for the level that should be met.

The answer sheets provide helpful practice in recording answers on a separate document. The standard-format test includes questions that require lateral thinking, typical of the most challenging assessments.

Remediation suggested in the answers, referencing the *Revision Guide*, can be helpful for follow-up revision having completed the paper.

Continue your learning journey

When you have completed these *Practice Papers*, you can carry on your learning right up until exam day with the following resources.

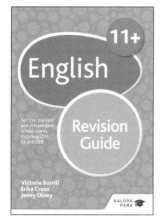   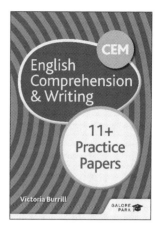

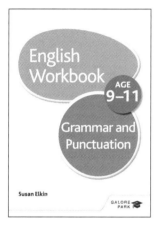 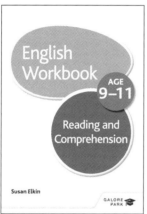  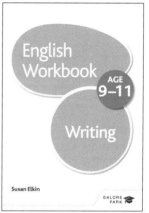

The *Revision Guide* (referenced in the answers to this book) reviews basic skills in all areas of English, and guidance is provided on how to improve in this subject.

Pre-test/11+ Practice Papers 1 and *2* are designed to provide a complete revision experience across the various test styles you may encounter. Between the two titles there are twelve model papers, each followed by writing tasks, and answers.

- *Book 1* begins with training tests, and contains a series of short papers designed to develop your confidence and speed.
- *Book 2* contains GL-style tests and bespoke papers intended for pupils taking the most advanced tests delivered at independent schools.

CEM 11+ English Comprehension & Writing Practice Papers contains four practice papers designed for preparation for the CEM-style tests. Each paper is split into short tests in comprehension; spelling, punctuation and grammar; cloze procedure; and writing. The tests vary in length and format and are excellent for short bursts of timed practice.

The four *Workbooks* (*Grammar and Punctuation*, *Reading and Comprehension*, *Spelling and Vocabulary* and *Writing*) will further develop your skills with 25 activities to work through in each book. These titles include more examples of the different types of questions you meet in these *Practice Papers* – the more times you practise the questions, the better equipped for the exams you will be.

Use Atom Learning to improve familiarity with online tests: the online learning platform adapts to your ability to ensure you are always working on your optimal learning path and the adaptive, mock-testing facility looks and scores in the style of the pre-tests.
galorepark.co.uk/atomlearning

Paper 1

Download and print the answer sheet from galorepark.co.uk/answersheets before you start this paper.

Part 1: Reading

Test time: 50 minutes

Read the text below carefully before answering the questions that follow it.

The Railway Children by E. Nesbit

Roberta, Peter and Phyllis and their mother have recently moved to Yorkshire after their father was mysteriously taken away from their home by two unknown men. Their life has changed dramatically as they now have little money. In this passage, the children are exploring the area around their new home.

So to the railway they went, and as soon as they started for the railway they saw where the garden had hidden itself. It was right behind the stables, and it had a high wall all round.

'Oh, never mind about the garden now!' cried Peter. 'Mother told me this morning
5   where it was. It'll keep till to-morrow. Let's get to the railway.'

The way to the railway was all downhill over smooth, short turf with here and there furze bushes and grey and yellow rocks sticking out like candied peel from the top of a cake.

The way ended in a steep run and a wooden fence—and there was the railway with the shining metals and the telegraph wires and posts and signals.

10   They all climbed on to the top of the fence, and then suddenly there was a rumbling sound that made them look along the line to the right, where the dark mouth of a tunnel opened itself in the face of a rocky cliff; next moment a train had rushed out of the tunnel with a shriek and a snort, and had slid noisily past them. They felt the rush of its passing, and the pebbles on the line jumped and rattled under it as it went by.

15   'Oh!' said Roberta, drawing a long breath; 'it was like a great dragon tearing by. Did you feel it fan us with its hot wings?'

'I suppose a dragon's lair might look very like that tunnel from the outside,' said Phyllis.

But Peter said:—

'I never thought we should ever get as near to a train as this. It's the most ripping sport!'

20   'Better than toy-engines, isn't it?' said Roberta.

(I am tired of calling Roberta by her name. I don't see why I should. No one else did. Everyone else called her Bobbie, and I don't see why I shouldn't.)

'I don't know; it's different,' said Peter. 'It seems so odd to see ALL of a train. It's awfully tall, isn't it?'

25   'We've always seen them cut in half by platforms,' said Phyllis.

'I wonder if that train was going to London,' Bobbie said. 'London's where Father is.'

'Let's go down to the station and find out,' said Peter.

So they went.

30 They walked along the edge of the line, and heard the telegraph wires humming over their heads. When you are in the train, it seems such a little way between post and post, and one after another the posts seem to catch up the wires almost more quickly than you can count them. But when you have to walk, the posts seem few and far between.

But the children got to the station at last.

Never before had any of them been at a station, except for the purpose of catching
35 trains—or perhaps waiting for them—and always with grown-ups in attendance, grown-ups who were not themselves interested in stations, except as places from which they wished to get away.

Never before had they passed close enough to a signal-box to be able to notice the wires, and to hear the mysterious 'ping, ping,' followed by the strong, firm clicking
40 of machinery.

The very sleepers on which the rails lay were a delightful path to travel by—just far enough apart to serve as the stepping-stones in a game of foaming torrents hastily organised by Bobbie.

Then to arrive at the station, not through the booking office, but in a freebooting
45 sort of way by the sloping end of the platform. This in itself was joy.

Joy, too, it was to peep into the porters' room, where the lamps are, and the Railway almanac on the wall, and one porter half asleep behind a paper.

There were a great many crossing lines at the station; some of them just ran into a yard and stopped short, as though they were tired of business and meant to retire
50 for good. Trucks stood on the rails here, and on one side was a great heap of coal— not a loose heap, such as you see in your coal cellar, but a sort of solid building of coals with large square blocks of coal outside used just as though they were bricks, and built up till the heap looked like the picture of the Cities of the Plain in 'Bible Stories for Infants.' There was a line of whitewash near the top of the coaly wall.

55 When presently the Porter lounged out of his room at the twice-repeated tingling thrill of a gong over the station door, Peter said, 'How do you do?' in his best manner, and hastened to ask what the white mark was on the coal for.

'To mark how much coal there be,' said the Porter, 'so as we'll know if anyone nicks it. So don't you go off with none in your pockets, young gentleman!'

60 This seemed at the time but a merry jest, and Peter felt at once that the Porter was a friendly sort with no nonsense about him. But later the words came back to Peter with a new meaning.

Have you ever gone into a farmhouse kitchen on a baking day, and seen the great crock of dough set by the fire to rise? If you have, and if you were at that time still
65 young enough to be interested in everything you saw, you will remember that you found yourself quite unable to resist the temptation to poke your finger into the soft round of dough that curved inside the pan like a giant mushroom. And you will remember that your finger made a dent in the dough, and that slowly, but quite surely, the dent disappeared, and the dough looked quite the same as it did
70 before you touched it. Unless, of course, your hand was extra dirty, in which case, naturally, there would be a little black mark.

Well, it was just like that with the sorrow the children had felt at Father's going away, and at Mother's being so unhappy. It made a deep impression, but the impression did not last long.

75 They soon got used to being without Father, though they did not forget him; and they got used to not going to school, and to seeing very little of Mother, who was now almost all day shut up in her upstairs room writing, writing, writing. She used to come down at tea-time and read aloud the stories she had written. They were lovely stories.

80 The rocks and hills and valleys and trees, the canal, and above all, the railway, were so new and so perfectly pleasing that the remembrance of the old life in the villa grew to seem almost like a dream.

From *The Railway Children* by E. Nesbit, 1906

Comprehension

Now answer the following questions in relation to the text.

Mark your answers in pencil, putting a line through your choice, as instructed on the answer sheet.

1   Where were the children heading at the start of the passage?   (1)

    A   The garden

    B   The stables

    C   The railway

    D   The kitchen

    E   The bushes

2   What was the terrain like between the house and the track?   (1)

    A   An upward slope of short grass with occasional rocks and shrubs

    B   A downward slope of short grass with occasional rocks and trees

    C   A downward slope of overgrown grass with occasional rocks and shrubs

    D   A downward slope of overgrown grass with many rocks and shrubs

    E   A downward slope of short grass with occasional rocks and shrubs

3   As they neared the railway, 'The way ended in a steep run and a wooden fence' (line 8). Where were the children when they saw the first train?   (1)

    A   Behind the fence

    B   In front of the fence

    C   On the fence

    D   Up the hill

    E   On the track

4   On the way to the railway line, the children saw '… grey and yellow rocks sticking out like candied peel from the top of a cake' (line 7). What is this an example of?   (1)

    A   metaphor

    B   simile

    C   personification

    D   onomatopoeia

    E   exaggeration

17 How did the children first get the Porter's attention at the station? (1)

   A   They called out for him.

   B   They waited until he came out of his room.

   C   They rang the bell once.

   D   They rang the bell twice.

   E   They asked a question.

18 'When presently the Porter lounged out of his room ...' (line 55). What is another way of saying 'presently'? (1)

   A   A long time after

   B   A short time after

   C   Immediately

   D   Today

   E   Finally

19 What type of words are the following: 'temptation' (line 66), 'dent' (line 68), 'sound' (line 11), 'shriek' (line 13), 'purpose' (line 34)? (1)

   A   adverbs

   B   verbs

   C   nouns

   D   prepositions

   E   adjectives

20 '... we'll know if anyone nicks it' (lines 58–59). Which of these words is closest in meaning to 'nicks'? (1)

   A   steals

   B   damages

   C   touches

   D   notices

   E   breaks

21 What is another way of saying 'a merry jest' (line 60)? (1)

   A   A white lie

   B   A practical joke

   C   A humorous joke

   D   A warning

   E   A proverb

22 The passage refers to seeing 'the great crock of dough' (lines 63–64). What is a 'crock'? (1)

   A   A mound or pile

   B   A pot or basin

   C   A loaf

   D   A solid lump

   E   An oven or stove

23 Which is the best description of how the children feel about their father being away? (1)

   A   They are extremely sad.

   B   They used to be sad but the feeling has faded.

   C   They are glad he is gone.

   D   They were happy at first but now they are sad.

   E   Everyone is still upset apart from Peter.

24 In the passage, Mother is 'almost all day shut up in her upstairs room writing, writing, writing' (line 77). What effect does the repetition of the word 'writing' have? (1)

    A It shows she wrote three times.

    B It shows that she really likes to write.

    C It shows that when you write you repeat things.

    D It makes the word stand out.

    E It shows that she did a large amount of writing or wrote for a long time.

25 What type of word is 'aloud' (line 78)? (1)

    A adjective

    B noun

    C adverb

    D verb

    E preposition

26 The family's 'old life in the villa grew to seem almost like a dream' (lines 81–82). Why did this happen? (1)

    A Life in the old villa was so long ago that they couldn't remember it any more.

    B They wanted to forget about their old home because it was not a happy time.

    C The place where they had moved to was so pleasant and enjoyable that it made their old home seem almost unreal.

    D The place where they had moved from was so pleasant and enjoyable that it made their new home seem almost unreal.

    E They wished that they could move back to their old home so much that they dreamed about it.

Spelling

Some of these sentences contain spelling mistakes. Look at each question numbered 27–34 and decide whether it contains a mistake. Find the group of words that contains the mistake and mark its letter on your answer sheet. *If there is no mistake, mark 'N'.*

27 (1)

After several minutes	the train apeared	and then vanished	into the distance.	
A	B	C	D	N

28 (1)

There are many	modern vehicles	whose existance is thanks	to creative individuals.	
A	B	C	D	N

29 (1)

The naughty	boys climbed over	the fence but fell down	and were embarassed.	
A	B	C	D	N

30 (1)

The incredibly shiny	flash of the engine	was exhilarating but	apparently quite terrifying.	
A	B	C	D	N

31 (1)

Unfortunately, I definitely	left my most treasured	posession on the train	last Wednesday morning.	
A	B	C	D	N

32 (1)

When I travel through France	I am hopefull that	I can be accommodated	in the sleeper carriage.	
A	B	C	D	N

33 (1)

She was grateful for	the valuable experiance	she had when she	travelled on her own.	
A	B	C	D	N

34 (1)

Successful inventions	come from persevering,	receiving help and	committing to your ideas.	
A	B	C	D	N

Punctuation

Some of these sentences contain punctuation errors. Look at each question numbered 35–42 and decide whether it contains a mistake. Find the group of words that contains the mistake and mark its letter on your answer sheet. *If there is no mistake, mark 'N'.*

35 (1)

The steam locomotive	was invented in	the victorian era	and is considered	
A	B	C	D	N

36 (1)

to be one of the	most important	inventions of it's time.	Before trains were	
A	B	C	D	N

37 (1)

invented people could	not visit areas far	from their own	homes it took too long.	
A	B	C	D	N

38 (1)

Today we have	cars planes and even	motorbikes but life	is different now.	
A	B	C	D	N

39	Can you imagine	never having left	your own town or	village. This was	
	A	B	C	D	N

(1)

40	quite common in the	nineteenth century.	People simply couldn't	travel far or fast.	
	A	B	C	D	N

(1)

41	Nowadays we have	trains that travel in	excess of 250mph.	Wow. That's quite	
	A	B	C	D	N

(1)

42	different from the early	steam engine built	by George stephenson	to transport coal.	
	A	B	C	D	N

(1)

Cloze

Choose the word or group of words that completes each sentence (numbered 43–50) so that it makes sense and is written in correct English. Mark the box next to the letter of your chosen answer on the answer sheet.

43 It was moving day. Our belongings A were B had been C have been D are
  E is packed for three days already and the house looked like a cardboard city.   (1)

44 My brothers were crying because they wanted A they're B there C their
  D they are E our favourite toys   (1)

45 but nobody A knew B new C knowed D had known E knows which
  box they were in.   (1)

46 I A could have B could of C may have D wouldn't E should of tried
  looking for them but I was too exhausted. I hadn't slept for a few weeks.   (1)

47 Moving A isn't B weren't C wasn't D hasn't E hadn't my idea and
  I was nervous about it.   (1)

48 Mum said it would be fine A therefore B because C besides D although
  E and I heard her crying last night.   (1)

49 I questioned her about it but she A didn't want B doesn't want C isn't
  wanting D wasn't wanting E hadn't wanted to talk about it.   (1)

50 As for me, I will make the best of things A wherever B whatsoever
  C somewhere D whatever E there we go.   (1)

Part 2: Writing

Choose **one** of the following options to create a writing composition. Complete your writing on a separate sheet of paper. Mark your test using the Writing guidance grids on pages 46–47.

1 Write a short descriptive composition about a journey when you watched the landscape pass by through a window. You can choose which vehicle you are travelling in. Use your imagination to bring the journey to life. (15)

2 Write a short descriptive composition based on the picture below. (15)

Paper 2

Download and print the answer sheet from galorepark.co.uk/answersheets before you start this paper.

Part 1: Reading

Test time: 50 minutes

Read the text below carefully before answering the questions that follow it.

The Sea-Wolf **by Jack London**

The narrator, Humphrey van Weyden, is aboard a ship called the *Martinez* off the coast of San Francisco in America. The sky is foggy and the captain has just spotted a steamboat through the mist, heading directly for the *Martinez*.

The vessels came together before I could follow his advice. We must have been struck squarely, for I saw nothing, the strange steamboat having passed beyond my line of vision. The *Martinez* heeled over, sharply, and there was a crashing and rending of timber. I was thrown flat on the wet deck. I remembered the life-
5   preservers stored in the cabin, but was met at the door and swept backward by a wild rush of men and women. What happened in the next few minutes I do not recollect, though I have a clear remembrance of pulling down life-preservers from the overhead racks. This memory is as distinct and sharp as that of any picture I have seen. It is a picture, and I can see it now,—the jagged edges of the hole in
10   the side of the cabin, through which the grey fog swirled and eddied; the empty upholstered seats, littered with all the evidences of sudden flight, such as packages, hand satchels, umbrellas, and wraps; the stout gentleman who had been reading my essay, encased in cork and canvas, the magazine still in his hand, and asking me with monotonous insistence if I thought there was any danger; the red-faced
15   man, stumping gallantly around on his artificial legs and buckling life-preservers on all comers; and finally, the screaming bedlam.

The horror of it drove me out on deck. I was feeling sick, and sat down on a bench. In a hazy way I saw and heard men rushing and shouting as they strove to lower the boats. One boat lowered away with the plugs out, filled with women
20   and children and then with water, and capsized. Another boat had been lowered by one end, and still hung in the tackle by the other end, where it had been abandoned. Nothing was to be seen of the strange steamboat which had caused the disaster, though I heard men saying that she would undoubtedly send boats to our assistance.

25   I descended to the lower deck. The *Martinez* was sinking fast, for the water was very near. Numbers of the passengers were leaping overboard. Others, in the water, were clamouring to be taken aboard again. A cry arose that we were sinking. I was seized by the consequent panic, and went over the side in a surge of bodies. How I went over I do not know, though I did know, and instantly, why
30   those in the water were so desirous of getting back on the steamer. The water was cold—so cold that it was painful. The pang, as I plunged into it, was as quick and sharp as that of fire. It bit to the marrow. It was like the grip of death. The taste of

---

the salt was strong in my mouth, and I was strangling with the acrid stuff in my throat and lungs.

35   But it was the cold that was most distressing. I felt that I could survive but a few minutes. People were struggling and floundering in the water about me. I could hear them crying out to one another. And I heard, also, the sound of oars. Evidently the strange steamboat had lowered its boats. I had no sensation whatever in my lower limbs, while a chilling numbness was wrapping about my heart and
40   creeping into it. Small waves, with spiteful foaming crests, continually broke over me and into my mouth, sending me off into more strangling paroxysms.

The noises grew indistinct, though I heard a final and despairing chorus of screams in the distance, and knew that the *Martinez* had gone down. Later I came to myself with a start of fear. I was alone. I could hear no calls or cries—only the sound of
45   the waves, made weirdly hollow and reverberant by the fog. A panic in a crowd is not so terrible as a panic when one is by oneself; and such a panic I now suffered. Was I being carried out to sea? And the life-preserver in which I floated? Was it not liable to go to pieces at any moment? I had heard of such things being made of paper and hollow rushes which quickly became saturated and lost all buoyancy.
50   And I could not swim a stroke. And I was alone, floating, apparently, in the midst of a grey primordial vastness. I confess that a madness seized me, that I shrieked aloud and beat the water with my numb hands.

How long this lasted I have no conception, for a blankness intervened, of which I remember no more than one remembers of troubled and painful sleep. When I
55   aroused I saw, almost above me and emerging from the fog, the bow of a vessel, and three triangular sails, each shrewdly lapping the other and filled with wind. Where the bow cut the water there was a great foaming and gurgling, and I seemed directly in its path. I tried to cry out, but was too exhausted. The bow plunged down, just missing me and sending a swash of water clear over my head. Then the
60   long, black side of the vessel began slipping past, so near that I could have touched it with my hands. I tried to reach it, in a mad resolve to claw into the wood with my nails, but my arms were heavy and lifeless. Again I strove to call out, but made no sound.

From *The Sea-Wolf* by Jack London, 1904

Comprehension

Now answer the following questions in relation to the text.

Mark your answers in pencil, putting a line through your choice, as instructed on the answer sheet.

1   'We must have been struck squarely' (lines 1–2). What happened to the ship?   (1)
   A   It capsized.
   B   Another boat sailed past it.
   C   It drove straight into a rock.
   D   It was hit head on by another boat.
   E   It changed direction.

2 'I do not recollect' (lines 6–7). Which of the words below from paragraph 1 is closest in meaning to 'recollect'? (1)

    A eddy

    B encase

    C remember

    D see

    E happen

3 Which of these words is closest in meaning to 'distinct' (line 8)? (1)

    A obvious

    B far away

    C recent

    D clear

    E correct

4 '... littered with all the evidences of sudden flight' (line 11). What does the narrator mean by this? (1)

    A People had left behind rubbish when they left the cabin.

    B People had left their belongings behind when they evacuated the cabin.

    C There was evidence in the cabin of why the boat had been damaged.

    D The seats were covered in the kind of things people take on an aeroplane.

    E People had left their belongings behind to show which seat they were sitting in.

5 What was odd about the reaction of 'the stout gentleman' (line 12) to the events at sea? (1)

    A He wasn't immediately aware of the danger.

    B He didn't do anything.

    C He didn't help evacuate the boat.

    D He continued to read his magazine.

    E He put lifejackets on everyone but himself.

6 Which of these words is closest in meaning to 'monotonous' (line 14)? (1)

    A repetitive

    B fearful

    C urgent

    D annoying

    E anxious

7 What is another way of saying 'gallantly' (line 15)? (1)

    A quickly

    B clumsily

    C bravely

    D carefully

    E easily

8 Why did the narrator go out on deck? (1)

    A There were too many people inside.

    B He was going to vomit.

    C He needed to sit down.

    D He wanted to find a lifejacket.

    E He couldn't bear what he saw inside.

9 'In a hazy way I saw and heard men rushing and shouting as they strove to lower the boats' (lines 18–19). Which are the verbs in this sentence? (1)

   A way, saw, heard, rushing, shouting
   B way, saw, heard, strove, lower
   C way, saw, heard, strove
   D saw, heard, rushing, shouting, strove, lower
   E way, saw, heard, rushing, shouting, lower

10 The narrator mentions two lifeboats being lowered to the water. What happened to them? (1)

   A One filled with water and the other wasn't properly untied from the main ship.
   B One was filled with people and floated away but the other wasn't properly untied from the main ship.
   C Both boats were successfully launched but one capsized.
   D Neither boat was launched into the water.
   E One capsized as it had too many people in and the other wasn't properly untied from the main ship.

11 In the sentence 'I was seized by the consequent panic' (line 28), what type of word is 'consequent'? (1)

   A preposition
   B adverb
   C noun
   D pronoun
   E adjective

12 Which of these words is closest in meaning to 'surge' (line 28)? (1)

   A pile
   B crowd
   C group
   D rush
   E confusion

13 What did the narrator understand as soon as he hit the water? (1)

   A How cold it was
   B Why people wanted to get back onto the ship
   C How he had fallen into the water
   D That he was going to die
   E That the boat was on fire

14 'It bit to the marrow' (line 32). What does this metaphor mean? (1)

   A The water was so cold he could feel it in his bones.
   B The water was so cold he knew he'd die by the morning.
   C The water felt like it was chewing at his skin.
   D It was so cold his teeth were chattering.
   E It was so cold his limbs were shaking.

15 'The pang, as I plunged into it, was as quick and sharp as that of fire' (lines 31–32). What does this tell the reader about the water? (1)

    A The water was so painfully hot that it felt like it was burning his skin.

    B The water was so painfully cold that it felt like it was burning his skin.

    C The water was burning as the fuel had leaked from the boat.

    D He hit the water so hard when he fell in that it hurt him.

    E It was so cold that he couldn't escape from it, like being trapped in a fire.

16 Which of these words is closest in meaning to 'floundering' (line 36)? (1)

    A sinking

    B swimming

    C drowning

    D thrashing

    E waving

17 'I heard, also, the sound of oars' (line 37). Where was the sound coming from? (1)

    A The narrator's imagination

    B Lifeboats from the *Martinez*

    C Lifeboats from the boat that had hit the *Martinez*

    D The lifeboat the narrator was in

    E Local boats coming to the rescue

18 'Later I came to myself with a start of fear' (lines 43–44). What does this tell us about the narrator? (1)

    A He didn't know where he was.

    B He regained consciousness suddenly.

    C He gradually grew more afraid.

    D He woke up slowly.

    E He began to be afraid.

19 'Was I being carried out to sea? And the life-preserver in which I floated? Was it not liable to go to pieces at any moment?' (lines 47–48). What do these questions tell us about the narrator? (1)

    A That he was going mad and talking to himself

    B That he was curious

    C That he was confused and worried about his situation

    D That he clearly knew what to do next

    E That he wasn't very clever as he didn't know the answers

20 What is the narrator's main concern about his life-preserver? (1)

    A That it would unbuckle and float away

    B That it would absorb water and stop floating

    C That it would disintegrate in the water

    D That he was too heavy for it to keep him afloat

    E That he didn't know where it was

21 The narrator describes being 'in the midst of a grey primordial vastness' (lines 50–51). What does this tell you about the ocean? (1)

   A It is dark and cold.

   B It is dangerous and cold.

   C It is beautiful and deep.

   D It is misty and rough.

   E It is enormous and ancient.

22 'I shrieked aloud' (lines 51–52). What type of word is 'aloud'? (1)

   A adverb

   B adjective

   C noun

   D preposition

   E pronoun

23 'I confess that a madness seized me' (line 51). Which are the pronouns in this sentence? (1)

   A I and a

   B I and me

   C I, a and me

   D a and me

   E that and me

24 'How long this lasted I have no conception' (line 53). Why was this the case? (1)

   A He fell asleep.

   B He was unconscious.

   C He was in too much pain.

   D It was too dark.

   E It was too foggy.

25 What did the narrator see when he regained consciousness in the water? (1)

   A Nothing as it was too dark

   B Nothing as it was too foggy

   C Three boats in the water ahead

   D The back of a ship heading away from him

   E The front of a ship heading towards him

26 Which two of the following feelings does the narrator experience at the end of the passage? (1)

   i   happiness

   ii fear

   iii desperation

   iv anger

   v amazement

   A i and ii

   B ii and iii

   C ii and v

   D iii and iv

   E i and v

Spelling

Some of these sentences contain spelling mistakes. Look at each question numbered 27–34 and decide whether each contains a mistake. Find the group of words that contains the mistake and mark its letter on your answer sheet. *If there is no mistake, mark 'N'.*

27

In poor weather conditions,	life on the ocean	can be exilerating	or it can be terrifying.	
A	B	C	D	N

(1)

28

In principal, sailing	is a simple way to travel	from place to place although	it requires skilful manoeuvres.	
A	B	C	D	N

(1)

29

Sailing around the world	is an ambitious undertaking	that takes commitment,	knowledge, confidence and bravery.	
A	B	C	D	N

(1)

30

The coastguard is frequently	called to the assistence	of various vessels facing	possible disaster at sea.	
A	B	C	D	N

(1)

31

On foggy days it is	difficult to perceive distances	accurately so precede	with adequate caution.	
A	B	C	D	N

(1)

32

The bright flashes of	lightning and the uneven	rhythmn of the thunder	frightened the sailors.	
A	B	C	D	N

(1)

33

Many different vehicles	transport people and products	at sea including yachts,	cruise liners and cargo ships.	
A	B	C	D	N

(1)

34

Sailing is an excellent way to	occupy yourself on holiday	but don't fall overboard as	it would prove embarassing.	
A	B	C	D	N

(1)

Punctuation

Some of these sentences contain punctuation errors. Look at each question numbered 35–42 and decide whether it contains a mistake. Find the group of words that contains the mistake and mark its letter on your answer sheet. *If there is no mistake, mark 'N'.*

Sailing solo

35 (1)

An internationally known sportswoman,	dame Ellen MacArthur	is a female yachtswoman	who	
A	B	C	D	N

36 (1)

broke the world record	for the fastest solo	circumnavigation of the world.	She did this in	
A	B	C	D	N

37 (1)

February 2005,	although the record was broken again	three years later.	Her boat was called the	
A	B	C	D	N

38 (1)

castorama and	she completed the journey	in 71 days and 14 hours.	During that time she had	
A	B	C	D	N

39 (1)

no more than	20 minutes sleep at a time;	as she had to be on constant lookout.	So why would	
A	B	C	D	N

40 (1)

anyone want to take on	such an enormous challenge.	In an interview,	she told a reporter,	
A	B	C	D	N

41 (1)

'Its about going out there	and competing.' It was a trip	on her aunt's sailing boat	aged four years old	
A	B	C	D	N

42	that sparked her interest	in sailing she spent some of her	pocket money on sailing magazines	and saved the rest to buy a boat.		(1)
	A	B	C	D	N	

Cloze

Choose the word or group of words that completes each sentence (numbered 43–50) so that it makes sense and is written in correct English. Mark the box next to the letter of your chosen answer on the answer sheet.

43 The largest ship in the world A was built B built C was building
    D has been built E had been built in 1979 and was called *Seawise Giant*.   (1)

44 To follow in Ellen MacArthur's footsteps, you A might B should C would
    D must E can need to sail over 50,000 km.   (1)

45 British sailors A win B are winning C has won D wins E have won
    a number of medals in sailing at the last two Olympic Games.   (1)

46 The sailors didn't know A if B weather C whether D which E where
    or not to return to port when the storm began.   (1)

47 My brother is afraid of the water so Mum asked if I could fetch A her B his
    C my D him E its toy boat from the sea.   (1)

48 The boat was prevented from coming to shore A although B when C due to
    D but E as the high winds.   (1)

49 When we saw the bad weather forecast, we shouldn't A of B have C not
    D has E off continued our journey.   (1)

50 We have been rowing this boat A from B since C for D near E in
    two hours.   (1)

Part 2: Writing   Test time: 45 minutes

Complete both writing tasks in this section on a separate sheet of paper.
Mark your test using the Writing guidance grids on pages 49–50.

1 Write a story about being at sea during a storm. Use all of your senses to
    bring the weather to life.   (15)

2 Write a diary entry about making a journey across or through water. Choose
    which character you will be – the ship's captain, a sailor, a passenger or even
    a stowaway.   (15)

Paper 3

Download and print the answer sheet from galorepark.co.uk/answersheets before you start this paper.

Part 1: Reading

Test time: 50 minutes

Read the text below carefully before answering the questions that follow it.

One Flew into the Cuckoo's Egg by Bill Oddie

This extract is from the presenter, naturalist and birdwatcher Bill Oddie's autobiography. In this part he tells tales of his childhood antics, playing with friends.

St Alban's churchyard was particularly suited to games which entailed hiding, since quite a few of the graves were open! Several of what on the face of it appeared to be concrete tombs appeared to have missing lids or collapsed sides, so kid logic told you that there ought to be a dead body in there, and if there wasn't it had either
5   been stolen or had transformed into a zombie.

Inevitably, kids spooked themselves and one another by daring to peer inside. It was also unthinkable that any new kid on the block would not have been told tales of skulls, skeletons, ghosts and ghouls. Since I wasn't actually born in St Alban's Terrace, I myself must have been the victim of such teasing when I'd first gone
10 out to play with the locals at the age of – what was I? – I presume four or five. It certainly worked! If I do my close-my-eyes trick and think back, I can see the cold, grey churchyard, and the equally cold, grey tomb, one of which has the lid half missing. I am alone, as if abandoned. As if my mates have suddenly left me. Maybe we were playing 'hide and seek' and I was 'it'. I had closed my eyes and counted to
15 fifty, opened them and could see no one. Not in itself sinister. That was the idea of the game. I don't know if I searched far or for how long. All I remember – and I can see it now – is that my attention was drawn to the presence of 'something' in that slightly open stone tomb. And then suddenly, as I stared, a hand emerged, then an arm – bare, white, disembodied, surely dead, and yet undead. And no
20 sooner had I seen it, than it had gone and I was left trembling and terrified. If I said I recall what happened next I'd be lying. Did I carry on playing hide and seek? I doubt it. Did my friends eventually reappear? I expect so. Did anyone else claim to have seen a spooky white hand? Probably. Did anyone own up that it was them playing an obviously pretty effective jape*? Of course not. All I do recall is
25 that from that day on, as I went to and from school, I hurried past the St Alban's churchyard as quickly as possible, and I didn't look up. I literally kept my eye on the ball. The tennis ball that I was tapping ever closer to the sanctuary of my home.

Except that on this particular afternoon my ball control let me down and the ball skittered away and rebounded off my very own front doorstep and rolled under
30 the privet hedge that skirted the length of St Alban's Terrace. Have you ever tried finding a dingy old tennis ball that has disappeared into the gloomy featureless abyss that is the 'inside' of a thick privet hedge? It ain't easy, especially if you didn't see exactly the point of entry. Anyone who has thrashed a volley over the fence at the tennis court will know this all too well: you think you've noted exactly where

35   it plopped down behind the bushes, but tennis balls can not only bounce and roll, once they are out sight of their 'owners' they are capable of scuttling and hiding entirely of their own accord.

So there I was, on my hands and knees, crawling literally inside the hedge where the bushes fuse into one big scratchy, twiggy tangle, that is almost as impenetrable as
40   the Vietnam jungle, or a roll of barbed wire, and just as painful as either. Ants bit my hands, and twigs lacerated my legs, as I groped around in the layer of dead leaves and detritus that is the carpet beneath any privets. Not only do tennis balls scuttle and hide, they can also bury themselves, so I had no choice but to search by feeling around, which meant that my fingers more than once got gashed by discarded tin
45   cans and bits of broken glass. I hasten to add that all this torture is something that I and every schoolboy then and since suffers any time they play ball anywhere near a hedge. It's what you put up with if you want to get your ball back. And of course that is one of the major credos** in a schoolboy's code of honour: you must always get your ball back. One of the very first sentences a schoolboy learns is, 'Please can
50   we have our ball back?' Having to ask someone really scary and angry is the worst thing, but no matter if it plops down a drain, drops onto live railway lines, lands in a Rottweiler's food bowl, or indeed, rolls under a privet hedge, it must be retrieved. But this time, honour was not going to be satisfied. I felt around for a long time, but I simply couldn't find that ball. But what I did find was much more intriguing.

From *One Flew into the Cuckoo's Egg* by Bill Oddie, 2009

*__jape:__ joke
**__credo:__ a statement of beliefs

Comprehension

Now answer the following questions in relation to the text.

Mark your answers in pencil, putting a line through your choice, as instructed on the answer sheet.

1   Why was the graveyard so good for playing hiding games?   (1)

   A   Because it was so large

   B   Because of the open graves

   C   Because of all of the hedges

   D   Because there were no adults there

   E   Because it was too frightening

2   What happened to children who were new to the area?   (1)

   A   They avoided the graveyard

   B   They were told to climb into the tombs

   C   They weren't allowed to play games with the other kids

   D   They were dared to go into the graveyard

   E   They were told rumours of supernatural events

3   Why is the word 'something' (line 17) in inverted commas?   (1)

   A   Because someone is speaking this

   B   Because it shows that it is a quotation

   C   Because it shows that it is sarcastic

   D   Because he doesn't know what the 'something' is

   E   Because it makes it stand out from the rest of the sentence

4 What kind of word is 'disembodied' (line 19)? (1)

A verb

B noun

C adjective

D pronoun

E adverb

5 What is the effect of the questions Oddie uses in lines 21 to 24? (1)

A They show that he isn't sure what happened next.

B They engage the reader's interest.

C They tell you what he did next.

D They describe his feelings.

E They confuse the reader.

6 'If I said I recall what happened next I'd be lying' (lines 20–21). What does Oddie mean by this? (1)

A He was in shock and didn't remember what happened.

B He has a terrible memory.

C It was too long ago for him to remember.

D The story isn't actually true.

E He doesn't wish to tell people what happened.

7 Which of these words best describes Oddie's feelings when he remembers playing hide and seek? (1)

A joyful

B concerned

C afraid

D confused

E relieved

8 Why did Oddie's tennis ball roll under the hedge? (1)

A The ball had a mind of its own.

B He tripped over his front doorstep.

C He threw it, aimed badly and missed.

D He dropped it when he was bouncing it.

E The wind blew it there.

9 What does the word 'abyss' (line 32) mean? (1)

A maze

B landscape

C empty space

D chamber

E large shrub

10 'Anyone who has thrashed a volley over the fence' (line 33). What does the word 'thrashed' tell you? (1)

A The ball was hit really hard.

B The ball broke the fence.

C The ball won the winning point.

D The ball moved slowly through the air.

E The ball soared very high.

11 'Tennis balls can not only bounce and roll' (line 35) or 'scuttle and hide' (lines 42–43). What else does Oddie say they can do? (1)

    A Roll further
    B Stop rolling
    C Roll back towards their 'owners'
    D Bounce higher
    E Bury themselves

12 'Twiggy tangle' (line 39). What technique has been used here? (1)

    A simile
    B onomatopoeia
    C alliteration
    D repetition
    E personification

13 'Almost as impenetrable as the Vietnam jungle' (lines 39–40). What technique is being used here? (1)

    A personification
    B metaphor
    C simile
    D alliteration
    E rhythm

14 What does the author mean by 'almost as impenetrable as the Vietnam jungle' (lines 39–40)? (1)

    A The hedge was as thick with vegetation as a jungle.
    B The hedge was as unfamiliar as a jungle.
    C The hedge was very difficult to find.
    D The hedge was as far away as Vietnam.
    E The hedge was as confusing as a jungle would be.

15 Which of these words is closest in meaning to 'detritus' (line 42)? (1)

    A soil
    B debris
    C wildlife
    D dust
    E foliage

16 Which of these words is closest in meaning to 'lacerated' (line 41)? (1)

    A tickled
    B gashed
    C scraped
    D wrapped around
    E blocked

17 What difficulties did Oddie encounter when he was in the privet hedge? (1)

   i   Biting insects

   ii   Sharp branches

   iii Poor visibility

   iv Cold

   v   Sharp pieces of litter

   A   i, ii and iii

   B   i, iii and iv

   C   ii, iii and iv

   D   i, ii, iii and v

   E   ii, iv and v

18 How did Oddie feel about having to scrabble about under the bushes to get his ball back? (1)

   A   He strongly disliked it.

   B   He accepted that it was necessary even though unpleasant.

   C   He really actively enjoyed it.

   D   He wanted someone else to do it for him.

   E   He liked showing off about retrieving the ball.

19 What kind of word is 'your' (line 47)? (1)

   A   past participle

   B   adverb

   C   possessive adjective

   D   proper noun

   E   possessive pronoun

20 What was the worst thing about losing a ball? (1)

   A   Having to ask a stranger to give it back

   B   Having to go somewhere dangerous to get it back

   C   Having to ask an angry person to give it back

   D   Getting muddy while searching for it

   E   Hurting yourself while searching for it

21 How do you know this extract is from an autobiography? (1)

   A   It is about a person's childhood.

   B   It is written in the third person.

   C   It is very descriptive.

   D   It recounts real events from a person's life.

   E   It is in the present tense.

22 Which of these is a fact (rather than an opinion)? (1)

   A   'I wasn't actually born in St Alban's Terrace' (lines 8–9)

   B   'Maybe we were playing "hide and seek"' (lines 13–14)

   C   'They are capable of scuttling and hiding entirely of their own accord' (lines 36–37)

   D   'Did I carry on playing hide and seek? I doubt it' (lines 21–22)

   E   'Kid logic told you there ought to be a dead body in there' (lines 3–4)

23 Which of these statements is most likely to be true? (1)

    A   Oddie saw a ghost in the tomb.

    B   One of Oddie's friends played a trick on him.

    C   Oddie won the game of hide and seek.

    D   Every schoolboy wants to get his ball back.

    E   There was a real graveyard at St Albans.

24 Should the reader believe that every word of what Oddie writes actually happened to him? (1)

    A   Yes, because he should know what happened.

    B   No, because it's unrealistic.

    C   No, because he seems unsure about what he remembers.

    D   No, because it's fiction.

    E   Yes, because it's an autobiography.

25 What do you think is Oddie's main message in this extract? (1)

    A   Childhood is all fun.

    B   Childhood is frightening.

    C   Childhood is an adventure.

    D   Childhood is confusing.

    E   Childhood is difficult.

26 'But this time, honour was not going to be satisfied' (line 53). What does this mean? (1)

    A   Oddie did not find the ball.

    B   Oddie did find the ball.

    C   His friends would be annoyed.

    D   He would be in trouble for getting muddy.

    E   The ball wasn't important to him.

Spelling

Some of these sentences contain spelling mistakes. Look at each question numbered 27–34 and decide whether it contains a mistake. Find the group of words that contains the mistake and mark its letter on your answer sheet. *If there is no mistake, mark 'N'.*

27 (1)

Each bird flys	at different speeds	and in varied	formations in the sky.	
A	B	C	D	N

28 (1)

Flying high over	rooves and chimneys	birds demonstrate	both speed and elegance.	
A	B	C	D	N

29 (1)

Mother birds teach their	chicks how to fly,	watching as they are	carried by the wind.	
A	B	C	D	N

30

It is necesary for many	birds to migrate,	travelling south to hotter weather	weather to find food.	
A	B	C	D	N

(1)

31

When migration is successful,	birds return home in Spring	to build their nests	amongst the trees.	
A	B	C	D	N

(1)

32

Birds must be cautious	of the many predators	that threaten and catch	smaller, more vulnerable creatures.	
A	B	C	D	N

(1)

33

Some spieces of bird,	like pigeons and seagulls,	are found in cities	scavenging food from rubbish bins.	
A	B	C	D	N

(1)

34

Unfortunately, some birds	are facing exctinction	due to disturbances	to their natural habitats.	
A	B	C	D	N

(1)

Punctuation

Some of these sentences contain punctuation errors. Look at each question numbered 35–42 and decide whether it contains a mistake. Find the group of words that contains the mistake and mark its letter on your answer sheet. *If there is no mistake, mark 'N'.*

35

Migration is	the seasonal or regular	movement of birds	(and other wildlife from one part of the world	
A	B	C	D	N

(1)

36

to another they do this	to survive.	European swallows are	a particular type of bird that	
A	B	C	D	N

(1)

37	wouldn't survive the winter	without migrating.	Each september,	they fly south to warmer		(1)
	A	B	C	D	N	

38	climates in areas including	Africa the Middle East and India.	They can fly	up to 200 miles		(1)
	A	B	C	D	N	

39	a day,	mainly in the daylight	at up to speeds of 20 miles per hour.	Along the way, they may face		(1)
	A	B	C	D	N	

40	many dangers;	a number of birds	die every year	due to starvation or weather hazards.		(1)
	A	B	C	D	N	

41	Luckily,	swallows are fast enough	to avoid most predators.	One expert stated 'Rarely		(1)
	A	B	C	D	N	

42	do swallows suffer from	predator attacks.	Exhaustion is a	far more common risk to their safety.		(1)
	A	B	C	D	N	

Cloze

Choose the word or group of words that completes each sentence (numbered 43–50) so that it makes sense and is written in correct English. Mark the box next to the letter of your chosen answer on the answer sheet.

43 By the time winter begins, most birds   A   have left   B   leave   C   are leaving   D   left   E   had left   for warmer areas. (1)

44 An ornithologist is somebody   A   who   B   which   C   that   D   who's   E   whose   hobby or job is studying birds in the wild. (1)

45 When birds are young, they   A   are fed   B   were fed   C   feed   D   fed   E   would be fed   by their parents in the nest. (1)

46 Fledging occurs when baby birds   A   grows   B   grown   C   grew   D   grow   E   growth   feathers and are taught how to fly. (1)

47 If you had seen the documentary, **A** you will know **B** you knew
  C you could know **D** you would know **E** you shall know about parrots
  in the rainforest. (1)

48 Chicks hatch **A** from **B** for **C** by **D** inside **E** within eggs and are looked
  after by their parents. (1)

48 Some birds cannot fly because **A** there **B** their **C** they're **D** its **E** it's
  wings are not built to keep them in the air. (1)

50 Ducks often stand on one leg and can sleep with one eye open **A** to **B** too
  C two **D** tow **E** toe. (1)

Part 2: Writing

Test time: 40 minutes

Complete both writing tasks in this section on a separate sheet of paper. Mark your
test using the Writing guidance grids on pages 52–53.

1 Write an article for your school magazine, persuading people to give money to
  an animal charity. You can choose which charity you write about. (15)

2 Write a review of a fiction text you have read in which animals were very
  important. Make sure you include your opinion of the book and not just what
  happened in it. (15)

Paper 4

Part 1: Reading

Read the text below carefully before answering the questions that follow it.

The Hound of the Baskervilles by Arthur Conan Doyle

Sherlock Holmes is investigating the death of Sir Charles Baskerville and an ancient family curse. He learns that an escaped murderer, Seldon, is roaming the local area and he sends his assistant Watson out onto the moors at night to find him. Seldon is also the cousin of the Barrymore family, who have been helping him avoid capture. Watson, who is accompanied by Sir Henry, the Baskerville heir who has asked for the death to be investigated, is the narrator.

We stumbled slowly along in the darkness, with the black loom of the craggy hills around us, and the yellow speck of light burning steadily in front. There is nothing so deceptive as the distance of a light upon a pitch-dark night, and sometimes the glimmer seemed to be far away upon the horizon and sometimes it might have

5   been within a few yards of us. But at last we could see whence it came, and then we knew that we were indeed very close. A guttering candle was stuck in a crevice of the rocks which flanked it on each side so as to keep the wind from it and also to prevent it from being visible, save in the direction of Baskerville Hall. A boulder of granite concealed our approach, and crouching behind it we gazed over it at the

10   signal light. It was strange to see this single candle burning there in the middle of the moor, with no sign of life near it—just the one straight yellow flame and the gleam of the rock on each side of it.

'What shall we do now?' whispered Sir Henry.

'Wait here. He must be near his light. Let us see if we can get a glimpse of him.'

15   The words were hardly out of my mouth when we both saw him. Over the rocks, in the crevice of which the candle burned, there was thrust out an evil yellow face, a terrible animal face, all seamed and scored with vile passions. Foul with mire, with a bristling beard, and hung with matted hair, it might well have belonged to one of those old savages who dwelt in the burrows on the hillsides. The light

20   beneath him was reflected in his small, cunning eyes which peered fiercely to right and left through the darkness, like a crafty and savage animal who has heard the steps of the hunters.

Something had evidently aroused his suspicions. It may have been that Barrymore had some private signal which we had neglected to give, or the fellow may have

25   had some other reason for thinking that all was not well, but I could read his fears upon his wicked face. Any instant he might dash out the light and vanish in the darkness. I sprang forward therefore, and Sir Henry did the same. At the same moment the convict screamed out a curse at us and hurled a rock which splintered up against the boulder which had sheltered us. I caught one glimpse of his short,

30   squat, strongly-built figure as he sprang to his feet and turned to run. At the same moment by a lucky chance the moon broke through the clouds. We rushed over the brow of the hill, and there was our man running with great speed down the

35 other side, springing over the stones in his way with the activity of a mountain goat. A lucky long shot of my revolver might have crippled him, but I had brought it only to defend myself if attacked, and not to shoot an unarmed man who was running away.

We were both swift runners and in fairly good training, but we soon found that we had no chance of overtaking him. We saw him for a long time in the moonlight until he was only a small speck moving swiftly among the boulders upon the side

40 of a distant hill. We ran and ran until we were completely blown, but the space between us grew ever wider. Finally we stopped and sat panting on two rocks, while we watched him disappearing in the distance.

And it was at this moment that there occurred a most strange and unexpected thing. We had risen from our rocks and were turning to go home, having

45 abandoned the hopeless chase. The moon was low upon the right, and the jagged pinnacle of a granite tor* stood up against the lower curve of its silver disc. There, outlined as black as an ebony statue on that shining background, I saw the figure of a man upon the tor. Do not think that it was a delusion, Holmes. I assure you that I have never in my life seen anything more clearly. As far as I could judge, the

50 figure was that of a tall, thin man. He stood with his legs a little separated, his arms folded, his head bowed, as if he were brooding over that enormous wilderness of peat and granite which lay before him. He might have been the very spirit of that terrible place. It was not the convict. This man was far from the place where the latter had disappeared. Besides, he was a much taller man. With a cry of surprise

55 I pointed him out to the baronet**, but in the instant during which I had turned to grasp his arm the man was gone. There was the sharp pinnacle of granite still cutting the lower edge of the moon, but its peak bore no trace of that silent and motionless figure.

From *The Hound of the Baskervilles* by Arthur Conan Doyle, 1902

*__tor__: a hill or rocky peak
**__baronet__: a non-royal rank with the title 'Sir'

Comprehension

Now answer the following questions in relation to the text, writing your answers on the lines provided. Try to use your own words where possible.

1 What time of day was it at the start of the passage? (1)

_____

2 What is another way of saying 'whence' (line 5)? (1)

_____

3 In the first paragraph, the narrator describes 'the black loom of the craggy hills' (line 1). What does this suggest to the reader about the landscape? (2)

_____

4   Why was the candle 'stuck in a crevice of the rocks' (lines 6–7)?   (1)

_____

5   What is another way of saying 'concealed' (line 9)?   (1)

_____

6   'The words were hardly out of my mouth when we both saw him' (line 15). Describe
    in your own words the man that Watson and Sir Henry saw.   (4)

_____

_____

_____

_____

7   The man looked 'like a crafty and savage animal who has heard the steps of the
    hunters' (lines 21–22). What technique has been used here?

_____ (1)

8   'I sprang forward therefore' (line 27). Why did Watson do this?   (2)

_____

_____

9   What did the man do after Watson and Sir Henry jumped out of their hiding place? (2)

_____

_____

10 'At the same moment by a lucky chance the moon broke through the clouds'
    (lines 30–31). Which are the nouns in this sentence?   (2)

_____

11 In what tense and person is this story told? _____ (2)

12 Why does the author describe the man like 'a mountain goat' (lines 33–34)?   (1)

_____

_____

13 Watson did not use his revolver when he was chasing the man down the hill. What
does this tell you about him?   (2)

_____

_____

14 Find a phrase in paragraph 6 that shows that the man was quicker than Watson and
Sir Henry.   (1)

_____

15 '... at this moment that there occurred a most strange and unexpected thing'
(lines 43–44). Explain in your own words what it was.   (2)

_____

_____

16 What is another way of saying 'the jagged pinnacle' (lines 45–46)?   (2)

_____

17 'Do not think that it was a delusion' (line 48). What does Watson mean by this?   (1)

_____

18 'I assure you that I have never in my life seen anything more clearly' (lines 48–49).

What kind of word is 'clearly'? _____   (1)

19 How did Watson know that this second figure was not the convict they were
looking for?   (2)

_____

_____

20 '... the jagged pinnacle of a granite tor stood up against the lower curve of its silver disc'

(lines 45–46). What was the 'silver disc'? _____   (1)

21 Who or what do you think the second figure might have been? Give a reason for
your answer.   (2)

_____

_____

22 '... as if he were brooding over that enormous wilderness of peat and granite which
lay before him' (lines 51–52). Find and copy the prepositions in this part of the
passage.   (2)

_____

23 Would you like to have joined the two men on this expedition? Give a reason for your answer.   (2)

_____

_____

_____

24 '... but its peak bore no trace of that silent and motionless figure' (lines 57–58). What is the meaning of the phrase 'bore no trace'?   (1)

_____

25 Find two different conjunctions in the final paragraph.   (2)

_____

26 How do you think Watson was feeling at the end of the passage? Give a reason from the text in your answer.   (2)

_____

_____

Spelling

Some of these sentences contain spelling mistakes. Look at each question numbered 27–34 and decide whether it contains a mistake. Find the group of words that contains the mistake and circle the letter below your chosen answer. _If there is no mistake, circle 'N'._

27 (1)

When going on	an expedition, it is	essential to take	the right equiptment.	
A	B	C	D	N

28 (1)

If the weather changes	on a mountain, you	could be in imediate	danger if unprepared.	
A	B	C	D	N

29 (1)

Conditions can be	very changable so	take sensible clothing	and sufficient food.	
A	B	C	D	N

30 (1)

You may need strong	muscles to conquer	the challenging terrain	and diffrent obstacles.	
A	B	C	D	N

31	Make sure you plan	a schedule for your	excursion and practise	your navigation skills.		(1)
	A	B	C	D	N	

32	Make a good judgment	about the timing of	your walk so that you	return prior to sunset.		(1)
	A	B	C	D	N	

33	If you don't communnicate with each other	to ensure everyone's safety,	there is no doubt your outing	will be disastrous.		(1)
	A	B	C	D	N	

34	Enjoy the beautiful	scenery and fresh country air	and remember to	take some photographs.		(1)
	A	B	C	D	N	

Punctuation

Some of these sentences contain punctuation errors. Look at each question numbered 35–42 and decide whether it contains a mistake. Find the group of words that contains the mistake and circle the letter below your chosen answer. *If there is no mistake, circle 'N'.*

35	The mans outline was visible	in the light of the silver moon.	Who was he?	His shadowy figure		(1)
	A	B	C	D	N	

36	began to disappear	into the distance.	Suddenly the clouds engulfed the moon	and the hill was		(1)
	A	B	C	D	N	

37	cast into darkness.	After a few moments,	the clouds receded.	Gone the man was gone.		(1)
	A	B	C	D	N	

38	'Its like he evaporated	into thin air,'	I whispered aloud to nobody.	As I looked around me,		(1)
	A	B	C	D	N	

39

I could only see	the outline of the hill the moonlight	reflecting on the dewy grass	and the darkness	
A	B	C	D	N

(1)

40

of the forest ahead.	I was intrigued by the mysterious man	but I knew	the hills were'nt safe at night.	
A	B	C	D	N

(1)

41

As I turned to head home,	I heard a noise.	The sound, which was getting louder	seemed like	
A	B	C	D	N

(1)

42

it was coming from	where the man had vanished.	I couldn't resist	taking a closer look now.	
A	B	C	D	N

(1)

Cloze

Choose the word or group of words that completes each sentence (numbered 43–50) so that it makes sense and is written in correct English. Mark the box next to the letter of your chosen answer on the answer sheet.

43 As they began to A ascend B ascent C ascending D ascended E assent the mountain, everyone was in high spirits. (1)

44 The children A where B were C wear D we're E ware excited to be visiting the highest mountain in Europe. (1)

45 To get back on the path, walk A threw B through C thorough D though E thought   the long valley until you reach the black gate. (1)

46 The walkers stopped for a rest as A his B they're C there D their E our legs were aching. (1)

47 When the Sun shines A bright B brighter C brightest D brightly E brighten   in the sky, everyone enjoys going for a walk. (1)

48 They A couldn't have B wouldn't have C shouldn't have D couldn't of E shouldn't of   imagined how difficult the climb would be. (1)

49 Everybody made it to the summit A accept for B except for C accept of D except of E accepting two of the younger walkers. (1)

50 Dark clouds gathered overhead but nobody had A brung B bought C brought D bringed E brang a waterproof jacket. (1)

Part 2: Writing

Complete both writing tasks in this section on a separate sheet of paper. Mark your test using the Writing guidance grids on pages 55–56.

1 Use the picture below as a starting point for a short piece of writing. This can be a short story or a piece of descriptive writing. Make sure your work is linked to the picture. (15)

2 Continue the story from the passage on pages 36–37. Make sure you explain what the two men do next and whether they encounter either of the men they have seen that night. Make it exciting and descriptive. Aim to write two or three paragraphs. (15)

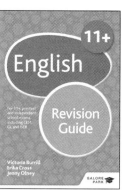

Answers

All the references in the boxes below refer to the *11+ English Revision Guide* (ISBN: 9781471849220) so you know exactly where to find out more about the question and your answer.

PAPER 1

Part 1: Reading

Comprehension

1	C	The railway	(1)
2	E	A downward slope of short grass with occasional rocks and shrubs	(1)

For more on improving retrieval skills, see pages 62–63.

3	C	On the fence	(1)
4	B	simile	(1)
5	E	personification	(1)

For more on improving analysis of language skills, see pages 71–75.

6	B	The train caused a rush of hot air.	(1)
7	B	He means that it's the most exciting thing to see.	(1)
8	E	The narrator	(1)
9	B	It seemed much larger because he could see all of the train.	(1)
10	B	To show that a letter is missing	(1)
11	B	Walking is much slower than travelling by train.	(1)
12	A	Present	(1)
13	E	Jumping from one railway sleeper to another	(1)
14	C	The lines came to an end so the trains couldn't travel any further and had to stop.	(1)
15	A	organised	(1)
16	C	ii and iii: There were many railway lines and The amount of coal was marked with a white line	(1)
17	D	They rang the bell twice.	(1)
18	B.	A short time after	(1)
19	C	nouns	(1)
20	A	steals	(1)
21	C	A humorous joke	(1)
22	B	A pot or basin	(1)
23	B	They used to be sad but the feeling has faded.	(1)

For more on improving inference and deduction skills, see pages 64–66.

24	E	It shows that she did a large amount of writing or wrote for a long time.	(1)
25	C	adverb	(1)
26	C	The place where they had moved to was so pleasant and enjoyable that it made their old home seem almost unreal.	(1)

Spelling

For general revision of spelling skills, see pages 14–23.

27	B	appeared not apeared – it should have two ps	(1)
28	C	existence not existance – it is an -ence word	(1)
29	D	embarrassed not embarassed – it should have a double r	(1)
30	N		(1)
31	C	possession not posession – it should have two double ss	(1)
32	B	hopeful not hopefull – words ending in -ful have only one l	(1)

For more on using suffixes, see pages 16–19.

33	B	experience not experiance – it is an -ence word	(1)
34	N		(1)

Punctuation

35 C   Victorian not victorian – proper nouns require a capital letter   (1)

For more on basic punctuation skills, see pages 24–25.

36 C   its not it's – possessive pronoun does not need an apostrophe (it's = it is)   (1)
37 D   homes. It took too long – the full stop and capital letter are missing   (1)
38 B   cars, planes and even motorbikes – comma needed in list of items   (1)

For more on using commas, see pages 26–28.

39 D   Can you imagine … village? – the full stop should be a question mark   (1)
40 N   (1)
41 D   Wow! That's quite … – the full stop should be an exclamation mark   (1)
42 C   by George Stephenson – proper nouns, including family names, need a capital letter   (1)

Cloze

43 B   had been – Our belongings had been packed   (1)
44 C   their – they wanted their favourite toys   (1)

For more on homophones, see page 22.

45 A   knew – but nobody knew which box they were in   (1)
46 A   could have – I could have tried looking for them   (1)
47 C   wasn't – Moving wasn't my idea   (1)
48 D   although – it would be fine although I heard her crying   (1)

For more on linking devices, see pages 118–119.

49 A   didn't want – she didn't want to talk about it   (1)
50 A   wherever – wherever we go   (1)

Part 2: Writing

What the examiners will be looking for:	Marks available: 15
Purpose and organisation: 1 Have you done as the task instructed? Have you spent most of your time on the main point behind the task? 2 Have you interpreted the theme imaginatively? Is your idea original and interesting? 3 Have you used paragraphs to separate the beginning, middle and end or to separate different ideas? 4 Does your opening sentence get the reader interested? 5 Is your last sentence a clear ending? 6 Is your composition definitely a description rather than a story?	6
Language: 1 Does your language match the genre you have chosen? Have you written in the first person if you are writing about personal experience? Have you used descriptive and poetic language in your description? 2 In your description, have you used plenty of interesting vocabulary? Check your choice of verbs ('ambled' tells us more than 'went'), adjectives and adverbs. 3 Have you used 'writers' tricks' such as metaphors and similes to make your writing more interesting and put a clear picture into the head of the reader? Have you used the senses for description?	4
Style: 1 Have you used a good mixture of simple, compound and complex sentences? Are your sentences of different lengths? 2 Have you used verb tenses correctly? (If you have started writing in the past tense, you should make sure that you have not drifted into using the present tense by mistake.) 3 Look at the first word of each sentence – do they all tend to be the same? If so, it will read rather like a list, so make changes to vary them.	3

What the examiners will be looking for:	Marks available: 15
Spelling, punctuation and grammar: 1 Have you used a range of punctuation including commas, exclamation marks, ellipses, speech marks? 2 Is your spelling of common words accurate? Is your spelling of complex words logical and reasonable? 3 Do your sentences make sense when you read them back? Are your verb tenses correct? Have you missed out any words? Have you written in proper sentences?	2

For more on how to respond to a textual prompt, see pages 93–94.

For more on responding to pictures, see pages 95–96.

Comprehension

1	D	It was hit head on by another boat.	(1)
2	C	remember	(1)
3	D	clear	(1)
4	B	People had left their belongings behind when they evacuated the cabin.	(1)
5	A	He wasn't immediately aware of the danger.	(1)
6	A	repetitive	(1)
7	C	bravely	(1)
8	E	He couldn't bear what he saw inside.	(1)
9	D	saw, heard, rushing, shouting, strove, lower	(1)
10	A	One filled with water and the other wasn't properly untied from the main ship.	(1)
11	E	adjective	(1)
12	D	rush	(1)

> For more on using clues to find definitions, see pages 60–61.

13	B	Why people wanted to get back onto the ship	(1)
14	A	The water was so cold he could feel it in his bones.	(1)

> For more on improving analysis of language skills, see pages 71–75.

15	B	The water was so painfully cold that it felt like it was burning his skin.	(1)
16	D	thrashing	(1)
17	C	Lifeboats from the boat that had hit the *Martinez*	(1)
18	B	He regained consciousness suddenly.	(1)
19	C	That he was confused and worried about his situation	(1)
20	B	That it would absorb water and stop floating	(1)
21	E	It is enormous and ancient.	(1)
22	A	adverb	(1)
23	B	I and me	(1)
24	B	He was unconscious.	(1)
25	E	The front of a ship heading towards him	(1)
26	B	ii and iii: fear and desperation	(1)

> For more on improving inference and deduction skills, see pages 64–66.

Spelling

27	C	exhilarating not exilerating	(1)
28	A	principle not principal – have different endings even though they sound the same	(1)

> For more on homophones, see page 22.

29	N		(1)
30	B	assistance not assistence – it is an -ance word	(1)
31	C	proceed not precede – watch for words with similar spellings but different meanings	(1)

> For more on prefixes, see pages 14–15.

32	C	rhythm not rhythmn – no n in this spelling	(1)
33	N		(1)
34	D	embarrassing not embarassing - two rs and two ss in this spelling	(1)

Punctuation

35	B	Dame not dame – capital letter needed for a person's title	(1)
36	N		(1)
37	A	No comma is required here	(1)

> For more on commas, see pages 26–28.

38	A	Castorama not castorama – capital letter needed for proper nouns	(1)

39 **B** No semi-colon needed here   (1)

For more on colons, semicolons and ellipses, see pages 32–33.

40 **B** Question mark needed after 'challenge'   (1)
41 **A** It's not its – this is an abbreviation of 'It is', not the possessive adjective for 'it'   (1)
42 **B** Full stop missing after 'sailing' and capital letter on 'She'   (1)

Cloze

43 **A** was built – The largest ship in the world was built in 1979   (1)
44 **C** would – you would need to sail over 50,000 km   (1)
45 **E** have won – British sailors have won a number of medals   (1)
46 **C** whether – didn't know whether or not to return to port   (1)
47 **B** his – asked if I could fetch his toy boat   (1)
48 **C** due to – prevented from coming to shore due to high winds   (1)
49 **B** have – we shouldn't have continued our journey   (1)
50 **C** for – We have been rowing this boat for two hours   (1)

Part 2: Writing

Writing guidance grid for Task 1

What the examiners will be looking for:	Marks available: 15
Purpose and organisation: 1 Have you done as the task instructed? Have you spent most of your time on the main point behind the task? 2 Have you interpreted the task imaginatively? Is your idea original and interesting? 3 Have you used paragraphs to separate the beginning, middle and end of the story? 4 Does your opening sentence get the reader interested? 5 Is your last sentence a clear ending? 6 Have you included some exciting action or events in your story?	6
Language: 1 Does your language match the story idea you have created? Have you used descriptive and poetic language in your story? 2 In your story, have you used plenty of interesting vocabulary? Check your choice of verbs ('ambled' tells us more than 'went'), adjectives and adverbs. 3 Have you used 'writers' tricks' such as metaphors and similes to make your writing more interesting and put a clear picture into the head of the reader? Have you used the senses for description? 4 Have you used dialogue? Have you described action? Have exciting events happened in your story?	4

What the examiners will be looking for:	Marks available: 15
Style: 1 Have you used a good mixture of simple, compound and complex sentences? Are your sentences of different lengths? 2 Have you used verb tenses correctly? (If you have started writing in the past tense, you should make sure that you have not drifted into using the present tense by mistake.) 3 Look at the first word of each sentence – do they all tend to be the same? If so, it will read rather like a list, so make changes to vary them. 4 Have you remembered to include the thoughts and feelings of characters (instead of just saying what they did and what happened to them)? Have you shown how they feel or respond through their actions, rather than just telling the reader how they feel?	3
Spelling, punctuation and grammar: 1 Have you used a range of punctuation including commas, exclamation marks, ellipses and speech marks? 2 Is your spelling of common words accurate? Is your spelling of complex words logical and reasonable? 3 Do your sentences make sense when you read them back? Are your verb tenses correct? Have you missed out any words? Have you written in proper sentences?	2

For more on writing from different points of view, see page 117.

What the examiners will be looking for:	Marks available: 15
Purpose and organisation: 1 Have you done as the task instructed? Have you spent most of your time on the main point behind the task? 2 Have you interpreted the task in an imaginative and interesting way? 3 Have you used paragraphs to separate the beginning, middle and end or to separate different ideas? 4 Does your opening sentence get the reader interested? 5 Is your last sentence a clear ending? 6 Have you written in the first person and past tense?	6
Language: 1 Have you used plenty of interesting vocabulary? Check your choice of verbs ('ambled' tells us more than 'went'), adjectives and adverbs. 2 Have you used 'writers' tricks' such as metaphors and similes to make your writing more interesting and put a clear picture into the head of the reader? Have you used the senses for description?	4
Style: 1 Have you included your feelings and emotions during the experience you have written about? 2 Have you used a good mixture of simple, compound and complex sentences? Are your sentences of different lengths? 3 Have you used verb tenses correctly? (If you have started writing in the past tense, you should make sure that you have not drifted into using the present tense by mistake.) 4 Have you written in the first person, opened with 'Dear Diary' and included a date? 5 Look at the first word of each sentence – do they all tend to be the same? If so, it will read rather like a list, so make changes to vary them.	3
Spelling, punctuation and grammar: 1 Have you used a range of punctuation including commas, exclamation marks, question marks and ellipses? 2 Is your spelling of common words accurate? Is your spelling of complex words logical and reasonable? 3 Do your sentences make sense when you read them back? Are your verb tenses correct? Have you missed out any words? Have you written in proper sentences?	2

For more on using imagery and description effectively, see page 110.

Part 1: Reading

Comprehension

1	B	Because of the open graves	(1)
2	E	They were told rumours of supernatural events	(1)
3	D	Because he doesn't know what the 'something' is	(1)
4	C	adjective	(1)
5	A	They show that he isn't sure what happened next.	(1)
6	A	He was in shock and didn't remember what happened.	(1)
7	C	afraid	(1)

For more on improving inference and deduction skills, see pages 64–66.

8	D	He dropped it when he was bouncing it.	(1)
9	C	empty space	(1)
10	A	The ball was hit really hard.	(1)

For more on improving analysis language skills, see pages 71–72.

11	E	Bury themselves	(1)
12	C	alliteration	(1)
13	C	simile	(1)
14	A	The hedge was as thick with vegetation as a jungle.	(1)
15	B	debris	(1)
16	B	gashed	(1)
17	D	i, ii, iii and v: Biting insects, sharp branches, poor visibility and sharp pieces of litter	(1)
18	B	He accepted that it was necessary even though unpleasant.	(1)
19	E	possessive pronoun	(1)
20	C	Having to ask an angry person to give it back	(1)
21	D	It recounts real events from a person's life.	(1)

For more on understanding purpose and structure, see pages 56–57.

22	A	'I wasn't actually born in St Alban's Terrace'	(1)
23	E	There was a real graveyard at St Albans.	(1)
24	C	No, because he seems unsure about what he remembers.	(1)

For more on recognising fact and opinion, see pages 69–70.

25	C	Childhood is an adventure.	(1)
26	A	Oddie did not find the ball.	(1)

Spelling

For general revision of spelling skills, see pages 14–23.

27	A	flies not flys – -ies ending for the third person singular of the verb 'fly'	(1)
28	B	roofs not rooves	(1)

For more on forming plurals, see pages 20–21.

29	D	carried not carryed – -ied ending for past tense of 'carry'	(1)
30	A	necessary not necesary – one c but double s in this spelling	(1)
31	N		(1)
32	N		(1)
33	A	species not spieces – watch position of the i in this spelling	(1)
34	B	extinction not exctinction – only one c in this spelling	(1)

Punctuation

35	D	The closing bracket has been omitted after 'wildlife'	(1)

For more on using parentheses, see page 29.

36	A	Full stop missing after 'another' and capital letter on 'They'	(1)
37	C	September not september – capital letter for proper nouns	(1)
38	B	Missing comma after 'Africa'	(1)
39	B	Missing parenthetical comma at end of clause after 'daylight'	(1)
40	N		(1)
41	D	Comma omitted after 'stated'	(1)
42	D	Closing speech mark missing after 'safety'.	(1)

For more on punctuating speech, see pages 30–31.

Cloze

43	A	have left – most birds have left for warmer areas	(1)
44	E	whose – somebody whose hobby or job is studying birds	(1)
45	A	are fed – When birds are young, they are fed by their parents	(1)
46	D	grow – Fledging occurs when baby birds grow feathers	(1)
47	D	you would know – If you had seen the documentary, you would know about parrots	(1)
48	A	from – Chicks hatch from eggs	(1)
49	B	their – Some birds cannot fly because their wings	(1)
50	B	too – Ducks often stand on one leg and can sleep with one eye open too.	(1)

For more on homophones, see page 22.

Part 2: Writing

Writing guidance grid for Task 1

What the examiners will be looking for:	Marks available: 15
Purpose and organisation: 1 Have you done as the task instructed? 2 Have you used paragraphs to separate each point? 3 Have you given an example to illustrate each point? 4 Does your opening sentence get the reader interested? 5 Is your last sentence a clear ending? 6 Have you introduced and concluded the piece of writing? 7 Have you written about events in chronological order?	6
Language: 1 Is your language clear and to the point? Remember that the opening sentence of each paragraph should clearly state the point you are making. 2 Have you used relevant vocabulary, specific to the topic? 3 Have you used time connectives (like 'then', 'finally' or 'eventually') to sequence events? 4 Have you used formal language? 5 Have you used persuasive language?	4
Style: 1 Have you used a good mixture of simple, compound and complex sentences? Have you varied the length of your sentences? 2 Look at the first word of each sentence – do they all tend to be the same? If so, it will read rather like a list, so make changes to vary them. 3 Have you used conjunctions to link ideas together within and between paragraphs?	3
Spelling, punctuation and grammar: 1 Have you used a range of punctuation including commas, exclamation marks, ellipses and speech marks? 2 Is your spelling of common words accurate? Is your spelling of complex words logical and reasonable? 3 Do your sentences make sense when you read them back? Are your verb tenses correct? Have you missed out any words? Have you written in proper sentences?	2

For more on writing persuasively, see pages 103–104.

Writing guidance grid for Task 2

What the examiners will be looking for:	Marks available: 15
Purpose and organisation: 1 Have you done as the task instructed? 2 Have you included details of your response to the book? 3 Have you backed up your opinions with examples? (If you like a particular chapter, give examples of why it was so good.) 4 Have you retold the entire story? Remember, you should not have done so! 5 Have you remembered to mention characters, plot, setting and structure? 6 Have you used paragraphs to separate each idea? 7 Have you used verb tenses correctly? (If you have started writing in the past tense, you should make sure that you have not drifted into using the present tense by mistake.)	6
Language: 1 Have you used clear, simple language to get across the points you want to make? 2 Have you used 'book' language (e.g. character, chapter, author, theme, etc.)?	4
Style: 1 Have you used a good mixture of simple, compound and complex sentences? 2 Look at the first word of each sentence – do they all tend to be the same? If so, it will read rather like a list, so make changes to vary them.	3
Spelling, punctuation and grammar: 1 Have you used a range of punctuation including commas, exclamation marks, ellipses? 2 Is your spelling of common words accurate? Is your spelling of complex words logical and reasonable? 3 Do your sentences make sense when you read them back? Are your verb tenses correct? Have you missed out any words? Have you written in proper sentences?	2

For more on writing book reviews, see pages 99–100.

Part 1: Reading

Comprehension

1   It was night time (1)
2   From where (1)
3   It suggests that the rocks were menacing / threatening / dangerous (1) and wild / weather-beaten (1).
4   To protect it from the wind **or** prevent it from being seen (1).
5   Hidden (1)
6   1 mark for each of the following, up to a maximum of 4 marks: frightening face, bestial, scarred skin, muddy, thick facial hair, knotted hair, sneaky eyes, looking around from side to side, like prey being followed. Note: Own words must be used although some nouns can be reused where no obvious synonym exists, e.g. eyes. (4)
7   Simile (1)
8   Watson knew the man suspected that someone was following him (1) and Watson thought he might disappear into the darkness at any moment (1)
9   The man shouted at them or 'cursed' (1) and threw a rock at them (1)
10 Moment, chance, moon, clouds (2). Award a half mark for each correct noun.
11 First person (1), past tense (1)
12 The man is agile on the hillside, and so like 'a mountain goat' is a suitable description (1)
13 1 mark for an adjective and 1 further mark for a reason, e.g. He is fair because he wouldn't shoot at a man who didn't have a gun to defend himself **or** He is well prepared because he brought a gun in case he got himself into danger. (2)
14 Either 'we soon found that we had no chance of overtaking him' **or** 'the space between us grew ever wider' **or** 'while we watched him disappearing in the distance' (1)
15 Watson saw the silhouette of a man (1) standing on top of the hill (1)
16 A rocky / craggy / pointed (1) peak / apex / crest / hilltop (1)
17 Watson means that he wasn't imagining what he saw (1)
18 Adverb (1)
19 He was far from where the convict had disappeared (1) and he was much taller (1)
20 The moon (1)
21 Any sensible suggestion with a reason, e.g. I think it was the ghost of somebody who died on the hills (1) because Watson says he was like 'a spirit' (1). Do not accept that it was Watson's imagination as the text clearly says it was not.
22 over (1), before (1)
23 Either yes or no. 1 mark for a simple reason; 2 marks for a reason that has been explained, e.g. I would not like to join the expedition because the hills sound frightening (1). I would not like to join the expedition because the escaped convict could be very dangerous and there is also another mysterious character on the hill who might be even more dangerous (2).
24 Showed no sign / exhibited no evidence (1)
25 Two from: and, as, but, besides (2)
26 Any sensible suggestion with a reason and quotation from the text, e.g. I think he was feeling confused (1) because the second figure had vanished so quickly – 'in the instant during which I had turned to grasp his arm the man was gone' – and he didn't know who or what it was (1)

Spelling

27 **D**   equipment not equiptment – verb equip + -ment ending (1)
28 **C**   immediate not imediate – double m in this spelling (1)
29 **B**   changeable not changable (1)

> For more on using suffixes, see pages 16–19.

30 **D**   different not diffrent – verb differ + -ent ending (1)
31 **N** (1)
32 **A**   In this sense, judgement not judgment – verb judge + -ment ending (1)
33 **A**   communicate not communnicate – double m but only one n in this spelling (1)
34 **N** (1)

Punctuation

35 **A**   man's not mans – apostrophe required before the s for a single noun (1)

> For more on using apostrophes, see pages 27–28.

36	C	Suddenly, the clouds – add comma after adverb to separate it from rest of sentence	(1)
37	D	Gone, the man was gone – add comma after first word to separate it from the main clause	(1)
38	A	It's not Its – not the possessive adjective for 'it' but the abbreviated form of 'it is'	(1)
39	B	Add semicolon after 'hill' to create a balanced sentence	(1)
40	D	weren't not were'nt – in contractions, the apostrophe is in place of the missing letter	(1)
41	C	Missing parenthetical comma at end of clause after 'louder'	(1)

For more on using parentheses, see page 29.

| 42 | N | | (1) |

Cloze

43	A	ascend – As they began to ascend the mountain	(1)
44	B	were – The children were excited	(1)
45	B	through – To get back on the path, walk through the long valley	(1)

For more on homophones, see page 22.

| 46 | D | their – The walkers stopped for a rest as their legs were aching | (1) |
| 47 | D | brightly – When the Sun shines brightly in the sky | (1) |

For more on using suffixes, see pages 16–19.

48	A	couldn't have – They couldn't have imagined how difficult	(1)
49	B	except for – Everybody made it to the summit except for two of the younger walkers	(1)
50	C	brought – nobody had brought a waterproof jacket	(1)

Part 2: Writing

Writing guidance grid for Task 1

What the examiners will be looking for:	Marks available: 15
Purpose and organisation: 1 Have you done as the task instructed? Have you spent most of your time on the main point behind the task? 2 Have you interpreted the visual prompt imaginatively? Is your idea original and interesting? 3 Have you used paragraphs to separate the beginning, middle and end or to separate different ideas? 4 Does your opening sentence get the reader interested? 5 Is your last sentence a clear ending?	6
Language: 1 Does your language match the task you have chosen? Have you written in the first person if you are writing about personal experience? Have you used descriptive and poetic language in a description or story? 2 Have you used plenty of interesting vocabulary? Check your choice of verbs ('ambled' tells us more than 'went'), adjectives and adverbs. 3 Have you used 'writers' tricks' such as metaphors and similes to make your writing more interesting and put a clear picture into the head of the reader? Have you used the senses for description? 4 If you have written a story, have you used dialogue? Have you described action? Have exciting events happened in your story?	4
Style: 1 Have you used a good mixture of simple, compound and complex sentences? Are your sentences of different lengths? 2 Have you used verb tenses correctly? (If you have started writing in the past tense, you should make sure that you have not drifted into using the present tense by mistake.) 3 Look at the first word of each sentence – do they all tend to be the same? If so, it will read rather like a list, so make changes to vary them. 4 Have you remembered to include the thoughts and feelings of characters (instead of just saying what they did and what happened to them)? Have you shown how they feel or respond through their actions, rather than just telling the reader how they feel?	3

Spelling, punctuation and grammar:	2
1 Have you used a range of punctuation including commas, exclamation marks, ellipses and speech marks? 2 Is your spelling of common words accurate? Is your spelling of complex words logical and reasonable? 3 Do your sentences make sense when you read them back? Are your verb tenses correct? Have you missed out any words? Have you written in proper sentences?	

For more on using verbs for effect, see page 116.

Writing guidance grid for Task 2

What the examiners will be looking for:	Marks available: 15
Purpose and organisation: 1 Have you done as the task instructed? Have you continued the story from where it ended? 2 Does your continuation make sense based on what has already happened? 3 Have you picked up small details from the text and included them in your continuation for consistency? 4 Have you used paragraphs to organise your work? 5 Have you used verb tenses correctly? (If you have started writing in the past tense, you should make sure that you have not drifted into using the present tense by mistake.) 6 Does your opening sentence get the reader interested?	6
What the examiners will be looking for:	**Marks available: 15**
Language: 1 Does your language match that of the story you are continuing? 2 When writing description, have you used some interesting vocabulary? Check your choice of verbs ('ambled' tells us more than 'went'), adjectives and adverbs. 3 Have you used 'writers' tricks' such as metaphors and similes to make your writing more interesting and put a clear picture into the head of the reader?	4
Style: 1 Have you used a good mixture of simple, compound and complex sentences? 2 Look at the first word of each sentence – do they all tend to be the same? If so, it will read rather like a list, so make changes to vary them. 3 Have you included dialogue and action?	3
Spelling, punctuation and grammar: 1 Have you used a range of punctuation including commas, exclamation marks, ellipses and speech marks? 2 Is your spelling of common words accurate? Is your spelling of complex words logical and reasonable? 3 Do your sentences make sense when you read them back? Are your verb tenses correct? Have you missed out any words? Have you written in proper sentences?	2

For more on improving story continuations, see pages 97–98.